The little book of
Classic
Cocktails

The little book of

Classic
Cocktails

hamlyn

First published in 2001 by Hamlyn,
a division of Octopus Publishing Group Limited, 2–4 Heron Quays, London E14 4JP
This edition first published in 2002

Distributed in the United States and Canada by Sterling Publishing Co., Inc.
387 Park Avenue South, New York, NY 10016-8810

British Library Cataloguing-in-Publication Data
A catalogue record for this book is available from the British Library

ISBN 0 600 60748 8

Printed in China

10 9 8 7 6 5 4 3 2 1

Notes for American readers

The measure that has been used in the recipes is based on a bar measure,
which is 25 ml (1 fl oz). If preferred, a different volume can be used
providing the proportions are kept constant within a drink and suitable
adjustments are made to spoon measurements, where they occur.

Standard level spoon measurements are used in all recipes.
1 tablespoon = one 15 ml spoon
1 teaspoon = one 5 ml spoon
Imperial and metric measurements have been given in some of the recipes.
Use one set of measurements only.

UK	US
caster sugar	granulated sugar
cocktail cherries	maraschino cherries
cocktail stick	toothpick
double cream	heavy cream
drinking chocolate	presweetened cocoa powder
icing sugar	confectioners' sugar
jug	pitcher
lemon rind	lemon peel or zest
single cream	light cream
soda water	club soda

SAFETY NOTE The Department of Health advises that eggs should not be
consumed raw. This book contains recipes made with raw eggs. It is prudent
for more vulnerable people such as pregnant and nursing mothers, invalids,
the elderly, babies and young children to avoid these recipes.

Contents

TOP SHOTS 8
From the White Lady, that inspired blend of gin and
Cointreau from the 1920s, to the Flaming Lamborghini,
1990s performance art in a glass, this chapter
contains some of the best drinks on record.

SUMMERTIME 38
Hot days require a special approach to drinking. Here
are long drinks with a tropical or subtropical ancestry,
such as the Singapore Sling and Planter's Cocktail,
and dazzling blends of spirits like Long Island Iced Tea.

EXOTICA 68
A good cocktail should transport the drinker far from
the mundane cares of everyday life. Stunning colours
and unusual ingredients add to the fun. This chapter
offers a selection of especially sophisticated drinks,
such as the Zombie and the Caipirinha.

Introduction

Ever since the trend began in the 1800's, cocktails have never been out of fashion and are as popular today as ever. James Bond's ability to impress the ladies with a Vodka Martini in hand (shaken, not stirred) made him one of Britain's most elegant bachelors.

But if you are like most people, you've sipped a Daquiri, knocked back a Rusty Nail or toyed with a Black Russian without a thought for the rich history and culture that caused the cocktail to be such an inspiration to bartenders worldwide.

The history of the cocktail is a contested story whose truth may never come to light. All over the world people have been experimenting with different combinations of drinks, both alcoholic and non-alcoholic, for centuries. The origin of the name 'cocktail'

itself is not certain, although several theories have been proposed. One concerns the owner of an American bar who had a large ceramic container in the form of a rooster into which he poured the leftover drinks. The less affluent could drink from this container, served from a tap at the tail, hence a 'cocktail'. Some say the quality of the concoction was always good after the English sailors had been in as there was a good mixture of rum, gin and brandy.

Another theory dates back to 19th century America and a Colonel Carter of Virginia. A 'cock' was a tap and the 'tail' was the last muddy dregs from the barrel. Colonel Carter was served the tail at his tavern one day and threw it to the floor in disgust. He is reputed to have said that from then on he would only drink 'cock tails' of his own design, and his choice was a mixture of gin, lemon, bitters and sugar. Whatever the origin of the word, the creation of the cocktail can be traced back to the 19th century. One of the first of the modern cocktails to be recognised was the Martini, whose origins come from an 1862 recipe for Martinez. This drink was created by 'Professor' Jerry Thomas, bartender at the old Occidental Hotel in San Fransisco, for a gold miner returning to his home in Martinez, a town 40 miles to the east. By 1900 the Martini was known across the USA and had even spread to Europe. Around this time a growing list of basic cocktails emerged and steadily gained popularity.

The cocktail was given a boost when the Prohibition laws were brought into force in the USA in 1920, making the manufacture or sale of intoxicating liquor illegal. This led to a healthy black market, with bootleggers such as Al Capone distributing moonshine nationwide. The quality of some of this moonshine was rather dubious and cocktails became very popular in the illegal bars and clubs that sprang up at the time, as a means of disguising its raw taste. Many of the classic cocktails we know today were invented during this period.

This book features the classics – those that have stood the test of time.

Sugar Syrup
This may be used instead of sugar to sweeten cocktails and give them more body. It can be bought, but is simple to make at home.

Put 4 tablespoons of caster sugar and 4 tablespoons of water in a small pan and stir over a low heat until the sugar has dissolved. Bring to the boil and boil, without stirring, for 1–2 minutes. It may be stored in a sterilized bottle in the refrigerator for up to 2 months.

Top Shots

Dry Martini
Daiquiri
Screwdriver
Whisky Mac
Brandy Manhatten
Brandy Sidecar
Pink Gin
White Lady
Rusty Nail
Collinson
Cosmopolitan
Gibson
Flaming Lamborghini
Algonquin
Brandy Sour
Old-fashioned
New Yorker
Salty Dog
Metropolitan
Napoleon

Dry Martini

5–6 ice cubes
¼ measure dry vermouth
3 measures gin
1 green olive, to decorate

The Dry Martini, which was invented at the Knickerbocker Hotel in New York in 1910, has become the most famous cocktail of all. Lemon rind is sometimes used as a decoration instead of a green olive.

Put the ice cubes into a mixing glass. Pour the vermouth and gin over the ice and stir (never shake) vigorously and evenly without splashing, then strain into a chilled cocktail glass. Serve with a green olive.

Serves 1

Daiquiri

cracked ice cubes
juice of 2 limes
1 teaspoon sugar syrup
(see page 7)
3 measures white rum

**The Daiquiri was created
by an American mining
engineer working in Cuba
in 1896. He was expecting
VIP guests and his supplies
of gin had run dry so
he experimented with
rum – the result is this
classic cocktail.**

Put plenty of cracked ice into a
cocktail shaker. Pour the lime
juice, sugar syrup and rum over
the ice. Shake thoroughly until a
frost forms on the outside of the
shaker, then strain into a chilled
cocktail glass.

Serves 1

Screwdriver

2–3 ice cubes
1 measure vodka
2 measures orange juice

Put the ice cubes into a tall glass. Add the vodka and orange juice, and stir lightly.

Serves 1

Variation

To make a Greyhound, substitute grapefruit juice for the orange juice.

Whisky Mac

2–3 ice cubes
1 measure Scotch
   whisky
1 measure ginger wine

Place the ice cubes in a large
tumbler or old-fashioned glass.
Pour the whisky and ginger wine
over the ice, and stir lightly.

Serves 1

Brandy Manhattan

4–5 ice cubes
1 measure sweet
    vermouth
3 measures brandy
cocktail cherry

Put the ice cubes into a mixing glass. Pour the vermouth and brandy over the ice and stir vigorously. Pour into a chilled glass and add a cocktail cherry.

Serves 1

Brandy Sidecar

4–5 ice cubes
juice of 1 lemon
1 measure Cointreau
2 measures brandy

to decorate
orange rind spiral
cocktail cherry

**This cocktail dates back
to the First World War.
It was made for a man
who travelled to a Paris
bar in a chauffeur-driven
motorcycle sidecar.**

Put the ice cubes into a mixing
glass. Pour the lemon juice,
Cointreau and brandy over the
ice and stir vigorously. Strain into
a chilled cocktail glass. Decorate
with an orange rind spiral and a
cocktail cherry on a cocktail stick.

Serves 1

White Lady

2 measures gin
1 measure Cointreau
1 teaspoon lemon juice
about ½ teaspoon egg
    white
lemon rind spiral,
    to decorate

Place the gin, Cointreau, lemon juice and egg white in a cocktail shaker. Shake to mix, then strain into a cocktail glass. Decorate with the lemon rind spiral.

Serves 1

Pink Gin

1–4 dashes Angostura
    bitters
1 measure gin
iced water

Shake the bitters, to taste, into a cocktail glass and roll it around until the sides are well coated. Add the gin, then top up with iced water.

Serves 1

Rusty Nail

2–3 ice cubes
1 measure Scotch
    whisky
½ measure Drambuie
lemon rind spiral, to
    decorate

**Drambuie is a Scotch
whisky liqueur flavoured
with heather, honey and
herbs. It is said to be made
according to a recipe from
Bonnie Prince Charlie.**

Put the ice into a small tumbler
and pour the whisky over. Pour
the Drambuie over the back of a
teaspoon on top of the whisky.
Decorate the rim of the glass
with the lemon rind spiral.

Serves 1

Collinson

3 cracked ice cubes
1 dash orange bitters
1 measure gin
½ measure dry vermouth
¼ measure kirsch
1 piece of lemon rind

to decorate
½ strawberry
lemon slice

Put the ice cubes into a mixing glass, then add the bitters, gin, vermouth and kirsch. Stir well, then strain into a cocktail glass. Squeeze the zest from the lemon rind over the surface and decorate the rim of the glass with the strawberry and lemon slice.

Serves 1

Cosmopolitan

1 measure vodka
½ measure Cointreau
1 measure cranberry
    juice
juice of ½ lime
lime slice, to decorate

Pour the vodka, Cointreau, cranberry and lime juices into a cocktail shaker. Shake well. Strain into a cocktail glass and decorate with a lime slice.

Serves 1

Gibson

2 measures gin
a few drops dry
　　vermouth
1 cocktail onion, to
　　decorate

Combine the gin and vermouth
in a cocktail glass and stir well.
Decorate with the cocktail onion.

Serves 1

Flaming Lamborghini

1 measure Kahlúa
1 measure Sambuca
1 measure Bailey's Irish
    Cream
1 measure blue Curaçao

Pour the Kahlúa into a warmed cocktail glass. Gently pour half a measure of Sambuca over the back of a spoon into the cocktail glass, to create a separate layer on top. Pour the Bailey's and the blue Curaçao into two short glasses. Next, pour the remaining Sambuca into a warmed wine glass and carefully set it alight with a match. Pour it into the cocktail glass with care. Pour the Bailey's and Curaçao into the lighted cocktail glass at the same time. Drink with a straw.

Serves 1

Algonquin

4–5 ice cubes
1 measure pineapple
 juice
1 measure dry vermouth
3 measures Bourbon or
 Scotch whisky

Put the ice cubes into a mixing glass. Pour the pineapple juice, vermouth and whisky over the ice. Stir vigorously, until nearly frothy, then strain into a chilled cocktail glass. Serve decorated with a cocktail parasol and drink with a straw.

Serves 1

Brandy Sour

4–5 ice cubes
3 drops Angostura bitters
juice of ½ lemon
3 measures brandy
1 teaspoon sugar syrup
(see page 7)
lemon slices, to decorate

Put the ice cubes into a cocktail shaker. Shake the bitters over the ice, add the lemon juice, brandy and sugar syrup and shake until a frost forms on the outside of the shaker. Strain into a glass and decorate with lemon slices on a cocktail stick. Serve with a straw.

Serves 1

Variation

Whiskey Sour is also a classic cocktail – made with Bourbon whiskey instead of the brandy.

Old-fashioned

2 measures Bourbon
   whiskey
a few drops of sugar
   syrup (see page 7)
3–4 dashes Angostura
   bitters

to decorate
orange slice
cocktail cherry

Combine the ingredients in a tumbler and stir. Decorate with an orange slice and a cocktail cherry.

Serves 1

New Yorker

2–3 cracked ice cubes
1 measure Scotch
   whisky
1 teaspoon lime juice
1 teaspoon caster sugar
1 piece of lemon rind
lemon rind spiral, to
   decorate

Put the ice cubes into a cocktail shaker and add the whisky, lime juice and sugar. Shake until a frost forms on the outside of the shaker. Strain into a tumbler. Squeeze the zest from the lemon rind over the surface and decorate the rim with a lemon rind spiral.

Serves 1

Salty Dog

2–3 ice cubes
pinch of salt
1 measure gin
2–2½ measures
    grapefruit juice
orange slice, to decorate

Put the ice cubes into a glass. Put the salt on the ice and add the gin and grapefruit juice. Stir gently and serve, decorated with a orange slice.

Serves 1

Variation

Although traditionally a gin-based cocktail, Salty Dog can also be made with vodka instead. The rim of the glass can be frosted with salt, like a Margarita, for extra sparkle.

Metropolitan

3 cracked ice cubes
1 measure brandy
1 measure sweet
    vermouth
½ teaspoon sugar syrup
    (see page 7)
3–4 dashes Angostura
    bitters

Put all the ingredients into a
cocktail shaker and shake well.
Strain into a cocktail glass.

Serves 1

Napoleon

3 cracked ice cubes
2 measures gin
dash Dubonnet
dash Curaçao
dash Fernet Branca

Put all the ingredients into a
cocktail shaker and shake well.
Strain into a cocktail glass.

Serves 1

Summertime

Gin Sling

4–5 ice cubes

juice of ½ lemon

1 measure cherry brandy

3 measures gin

soda water

fresh cherries, to
    decorate (optional)

Put the ice cubes into a cocktail shaker. Pour the lemon juice, cherry brandy and gin over the ice and shake until a frost forms on the outside of the shaker. Pour, without straining, into a hurricane glass and top up with soda water. Decorate with cherries, if liked, and serve with straws.

Serves 1

John Collins

5–6 ice cubes
1 teaspoon sugar syrup
    (see page 7)
1 measure lemon juice
3 measures gin
1 lemon slice
1 mint sprig
soda water

Put the ice cubes into a cocktail shaker. Pour in the sugar syrup, lemon juice and gin and shake vigorously until a frost forms on the outside of the shaker. Pour, without straining, into a Collins glass. Add the lemon and mint and top up with soda water. Stir gently and serve.

Serves 1

Between the Sheets

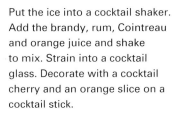

2–3 cracked ice cubes
½ measure brandy
½ measure white rum
½ measure Cointreau
1 tablespoon orange
    juice

to decorate
cocktail cherry
orange slice

Put the ice into a cocktail shaker.
Add the brandy, rum, Cointreau
and orange juice and shake
to mix. Strain into a cocktail
glass. Decorate with a cocktail
cherry and an orange slice on a
cocktail stick.

Serves 1

Long Island Iced Tea

12 ice cubes
½ measure gin
½ measure vodka
½ measure white rum
½ measure tequila
½ measure Cointreau
1 measure lemon juice
½ teaspoon sugar syrup
   (see page 7)
coca-cola
lemon slice, to decorate

Put half of the ice cubes into a mixing glass. Add the gin, vodka, rum, tequila, Cointreau, lemon juice and sugar syrup. Stir well, then strain into a tall glass almost filled with the remaining ice cubes. Top up with coca-cola and decorate with the lemon slice.

Serves 1

Moscow Mule

3–4 cracked ice cubes
2 measures vodka
juice of 2 limes
ginger beer
lime and orange slices,
    to decorate

This drink is one of those happy accidents. It was invented in 1941 by an employee of a US drinks firm in conjunction with a Los Angeles bar owner who was overstocked with ginger beer. It was originally served in a copper mug.

Put the cracked ice into a cocktail shaker. Add the vodka and lime juice and shake well. Pour into a hurricane glass, top up with ginger beer and stir gently. Decorate with lime and orange slices and serve with straws.

Serves 1

45

Sea Breeze

1 measure vodka
1½ measures cranberry
   juice
1½ measures grapefruit
   juice
5 cracked ice cubes
lime slice, to decorate

This is one of those drinks which has changed considerably over the years. In the 1930s it was made with gin rather than vodka and with grenadine and lemon juice instead of cranberry juice and grapefruit juice.

Put the vodka, cranberry and grapefruit juices into a tall glass with the ice cubes and stir well. Decorate with a lime slice and serve with a straw.

Serves 1

Cuba Libre

2–3 ice cubes
1½ measures dark rum
juice of ½ lime
coca-cola
lime slice, to decorate

Place the ice cubes in a tall glass and pour over the rum and lime juice. Stir to mix. Top up with coca-cola, decorate with a lime slice and serve with a straw.

Serves 1

Beachcomber

crushed ice
1 measure crème de
   menthe
soda water or lemonade
mint sprigs, to decorate

Put the ice into a large goblet and pour over the crème de menthe. Top up with soda water or lemonade. Decorate with mint sprigs.

Serves 1

Harvey Wallbanger

6 cracked ice cubes
1½ measures vodka
125 ml (4 fl oz) orange
    juice
1–2 teaspoons Galliano
orange slices, to
    decorate

A drink from the 1960s, the Harvey Wallbanger is said to have been named after a Californian surfer who drank so much of it that, as he found his way out of the bar, he banged and bounced from one wall to the other.

Put half the ice cubes, the vodka and orange juice into a cocktail shaker. Shake well for about 30 seconds, then strain into a tall glass over the remaining ice cubes. Float the Galliano on top. Decorate with orange slices and serve with straws.

Serves 1

Bloody Mary

1 measure vodka
3 measures tomato juice
2 dashes Worcestershire
    sauce
squeeze of lemon juice
1 dash Tabasco sauce
ice cubes
salt and pepper
lemon slice, mint sprig
    or celery stick,
    to decorate

Put all the ingredients into
a cocktail shaker. Shake well and
strain into a tall glass. Add your
chosen decoration and serve
with straws.

Serves 1

Variation

If you do not have any
Tabasco sauce, add a
pinch of cayenne pepper.

Kir Royale

1 tablespoon crème de
    cassis
Champagne

Pour the crème de cassis into a
chilled tall glass or Champagne
flute. Pour in the Champagne and
stir until just blended.

Serves 1

Buck's Fizz

3 measures orange juice
3 measures Champagne
orange slices,
    to decorate

Pour the orange juice into a
chilled glass and top up with
the Champagne. Remember to
choose a glass large enough
to allow for the drink to bubble
up as the Champagne is added.
Decorate with orange slices.

Serves 1

Singapore Sling

1–2 cracked ice cubes
1 measure gin
¼ measure cherry brandy
¼ measure Cointreau
juice of ½ lemon
soda water

to decorate
pineapple slice
strawberry
orange slice

Put the ice into a tall glass. Add the gin, cherry brandy, Cointreau and lemon juice. Stir and top up with soda water. Decorate with the pineapple, strawberry and orange speared on a cocktail stick and serve with a straw.

Serves 1

Americano

4 cracked ice cubes
1 measure Campari
2 measures sweet
    vermouth
soda water
lemon slice, to serve

Put the cracked ice into a tumbler, pour over the Campari and vermouth and stir to mix. Top up with soda water to taste. Serve with a lemon slice.

Serves 1

Whisky Daisy

crushed ice
1 egg white (optional)
½ measure lemon juice
1 measure Scotch
    whisky
1 teaspoon Pernod
2 dashes grenadine
soda water
lemon rind spiral,
    to decorate

Put the ice into a cocktail shaker and add the egg white, if using, lemon juice, whisky, Pernod and grenadine. Shake to mix. Pour into a tumbler, top up with soda water and decorate with a lemon rind spiral.

Serves 1

French '75

6 cracked ice cubes
1 measure gin
juice of ½ lemon
1 teaspoon caster sugar
Champagne
orange slice, to decorate

Half-fill a tall glass with the cracked ice. Add the gin, lemon juice and sugar and stir well. Top up with chilled Champagne. Serve with an orange slice.

Serves 1

Planter's Cocktail

3 cracked ice cubes
1 measure dark rum
½ measure orange juice
½ measure lemon juice
2 dashes Angostura
    bitters
1 teaspoon caster sugar

to decorate
pineapple cubes
banana slices
orange rind spiral

Put the ice cubes into a cocktail shaker and add the rum, orange and lemon juices, bitters and sugar. Shake until a frost forms on the outside of the shaker. Strain into a cocktail glass. Decorate with the pineapple, banana and an orange rind spiral.

Serves 1

New Orleans

6 cracked ice cubes

1 measure white rum

2 teaspoons lime juice

2 teaspoons orange juice

1–2 dashes Peychaud's
    bitters

ginger ale

lime slice, to decorate

Put half the ice into a cocktail shaker and add the rum, lime and orange juices and bitters. Shake until a frost forms on the outside of the shaker. Strain into a cocktail glass, add the remaining ice and top up with ginger ale. Stir, and decorate with a lime slice.

Serves 1

Classic Pimm's

1 measure Pimm's
3–4 ice cubes
orange, lemon and
    cucumber slices
3 measures lemonade
mint or borage sprigs, to
    decorate (optional)

Pour the Pimm's into a hurricane or highball glass and add a few ice cubes. Add the fruit and cucumber slices, then add the lemonade. Decorate with mint or borage and serve with a straw.

Serves 1

Classic Champagne Cocktail

1 sugar lump
1–2 dashes Angostura
    bitters
1 measure brandy
4 measures chilled
    Champagne
orange slice, to decorate

Put the sugar lump into a chilled cocktail or Champagne glass and saturate with the bitters. Add the brandy, then fill the glass with Champagne. Decorate with an orange slice.

Serves 1

Mai Tai

lightly beaten egg white
caster sugar
2 measures white rum
1 measure orange juice
1 measure lime juice
crushed ice

to decorate
cocktail cherries
pineapple cubes
orange slices

Dip the rim of a tall glass into the beaten egg white, then in the caster sugar to frost it. Put the rum, orange and lime juices into a cocktail shaker and shake to mix. Put the ice into the glass and pour the cocktail over it. Decorate with the cherries, pineapple cubes and orange slices and serve with a straw.

Serves 1

Tom Collins

1½ measures gin
1½ teaspoons lemon
    juice
1½ teaspoons sugar
    syrup (see page 7)
3 cracked ice cubes
soda water
cocktail cherry, to
    decorate

Pour the gin, lemon juice and sugar syrup into a tall glass, stir well and add the ice. Fill the glass with soda and decorate with a cocktail cherry.

Serves 1

Virginia Mint Julep

9 young mint sprigs
1 teaspoon sugar syrup
    (see page 7)
crushed ice
3 measures Bourbon
    whiskey
mint sprig, to decorate

Making the perfect julep is time-consuming. Ideally it should be served in a chilled silver mug. Only crushed ice should be used and the mug mustn't be touched during the preparation, otherwise the frost will disappear. If you haven't got a silver mug, use a tall glass instead.

Put the mint sprigs into an iced silver mug or tall glass. Add the sugar syrup, then crush the mint into the syrup using a teaspoon. Fill the mug or a glass with dry crushed ice, pour the whiskey over the ice and stir until a frost forms. Wrap the mug or glass in a table napkin and serve decorated with a mint sprig.

Serves 1

Exotica

Egg Nog

Brandy Alexander

Black Russian

White Russian

Caipirinha

Sex on the Beach

Bellini

Grasshopper

Piña Colada

Tequila Sunrise

Brandy Classic

Luigi

Zombie

B-52

American Beauty

Acapulco

Egg Nog

4–5 ice cubes
1 egg, beaten
1 tablespoon sugar syrup
    (see page 7)
2 measures brandy
150 ml (¼ pint) full-fat
    milk
grated nutmeg, to
    decorate

Half-fill a cocktail shaker with ice.
Add the egg, sugar syrup, brandy
and milk and shake well for about
1 minute. Strain into a tumbler
and sprinkle with grated nutmeg.
Serve with a straw.

Serves 1

Brandy
Alexander

2–3 cracked ice cubes
1 measure brandy
1 measure crème de
    cacao
1 measure double cream
grated nutmeg,
    to decorate

**The most famous brand
of crème de cacao is Tia
Maria.**

Put the ice into a cocktail shaker
and add the brandy, crème de
cacao and cream. Shake well to
mix thoroughly and strain into a
cocktail glass. Sprinkle with
grated nutmeg.

Serves 1

Black Russian

4–5 cracked ice cubes
2 measures vodka
1 measure Kahlúa
coca-cola (optional)

Put the cracked ice cubes in a large tumbler or old-fashioned glass. Pour in the vodka and Kahlúa and stir gently. Top up with a little coca-cola, if using.

Serves 1

White Russian

5 cracked ice cubes
1 measure vodka
1 measure crème de cacao
1 measure full-fat milk or double cream

Put half the ice cubes into a cocktail shaker and add the vodka, crème de cacao and milk or double cream. Shake to mix. Put the remaining ice cubes into a tall narrow glass and strain the cocktail over them. Serve with a straw.

Serves 1

Caipirinha

6 lime wedges
2 teaspoons brown sugar
2 measures cachaça or
    vodka
4–5 ice cubes, crushed

This drink is made with cachaça, a Brazilian spirit made from rum and sugar cane.

Place 3 of the lime wedges in a large tumbler or old-fashioned glass and add the brown sugar and cachaça or vodka. Mix well, mashing the limes slightly to make a little juice. Top up with the crushed ice cubes and garnish with the remaining lime wedges.

Serves 1

Sex on the Beach

½ measure vodka
½ measure peach
    schnapps
1 measure cranberry
    juice
1 measure orange juice
1 measure pineapple
    juice (optional)
3 ice cubes
cocktail cherry, to
    decorate

Put the vodka, peach schnapps, cranberry juice, orange juice and pineapple juice, if using, into a cocktail shaker with the ice. Shake thoroughly. Pour into a tall glass, decorate with the cocktail cherry and serve with a straw.

Serves 1

Bellini

2 measures peach juice
4 measures Champagne
   or sparkling white
   wine
1 dash grenadine
   (optional)

to decorate
peach slice
raspberries

Mix all the ingredients in a
large wine glass and serve
decorated with a peach slice
and raspberries speared on a
cocktail stick.

Serves 1

Grasshopper

1 measure crème de
    cacao
1 measure crème de
    menthe
mint sprig, to decorate

Pour the crème de cacao into
a cocktail glass. Pour the crème
de menthe gently over the back
of a teaspoon so that it floats
on top and serve decorated
with a mint sprig.

Serves 1

Piña Colada

cracked ice cubes
1 measure white rum
2 measures coconut milk
2 measures pineapple
    juice
starfruit slice,
    to decorate

Put some cracked ice, the rum,
coconut milk and pineapple juice
into a cocktail shaker. Shake
lightly to mix. Strain into a large
glass and decorate with the
starfruit slice.

Serves 1

Tequila Sunrise

5–6 cracked ice cubes
2 measures tequila
150 ml (¼ pint) orange
    juice
2 teaspoons grenadine

to decorate
orange slice
starfruit slice (optional)

Put half the ice into a cocktail shaker. Add the tequila and orange juice and shake to mix. Put the remaining ice into a tall glass and strain the tequila mixture into the glass. Slowly pour in the grenadine and allow it to settle at the bottom of the glass. Decorate with the fruit and serve.

Serves 1

Brandy Classic

4–5 ice cubes
1 measure brandy
1 measure blue Curaçao
1 measure Maraschino
juice of ½ lemon
cracked ice
lemon wedge,
    to decorate

Blue Curaçao is a dazzling blue, orange-flavoured liqueur, made with the dried peel of the green oranges that come from the Caribbean island of the same name. It is also available in several other colours.

Put the ice cubes into a cocktail shaker. Pour in the brandy, Curaçao, Maraschino and lemon juice and shake together. Strain into a chilled cocktail glass. Add some cracked ice and a wedge of lemon and serve.

Serves 1

Luigi

4–5 ice cubes
1 measure orange juice
1 measure dry vermouth
½ measure Cointreau
1 measure grenadine
2 measures gin
orange slice,
    to decorate

Grenadine is an extremely sweet, bright pink, alcohol-free pomegranate syrup from France.

Put the ice cubes into a mixing glass. Pour the orange juice, vermouth, Cointreau, grenadine and gin over the ice and stir vigorously. Strain into a chilled cocktail glass, decorate with the orange slice and serve.

Serves 1

Zombie

3 cracked ice cubes
1 measure dark rum
1 measure white rum
½ measure apricot brandy
2 measures pineapple
    juice
1 tablespoon lime juice
2 teaspoons caster sugar

to decorate
cocktail cherry
pineapple wedge
mint sprig
caster sugar (optional)

Place a hurricane glass or tall glass in the freezer until the outside is frosted. Put the ice into a cocktail shaker, add the rums, apricot brandy, fruit juices and sugar. Shake until a frost forms on the outside of the shaker. Pour into the glass without straining. To decorate, spear the cherry and pineapple on to a cocktail stick and place across the top of the glass. Add the mint sprig and sprinkle the sugar over the drink, if liked. Serve with a straws.

Serves 1

B-52

½ measure Kahlúa
½ measure Bailey's Irish
 Cream
½ measure Grand
 Marnier

Kahlúa is a coffee-flavoured liqueur from Mexico.

Pour the Kahlúa into a liqueur or shot glass. Using the back of a spoon, slowly pour the Bailey's to float over the Kahlúa. Pour the Grand Marnier over the Bailey's in the same way. This will result in a three-layered shooter.

Serves 1

American Beauty

4–5 ice cubes
1 measure brandy
1 measure dry vermouth
1 measure orange juice
1 measure grenadine
1 dash crème de menthe
ruby port

to decorate
cocktail cherry
orange slice
mint sprig

Put the ice cubes into a cocktail shaker and pour in the brandy, vermouth, orange juice, grenadine and crème de menthe. Shake well and strain into a cocktail glass. Tilt the glass and gently pour in a little ruby port so that it floats on top. Decorate with a cocktail cherry, orange slice and mint sprig speared on a cocktail stick.

Serves 1

Acapulco

crushed ice
1 measure tequila
1 measure white rum
2 measures pineapple
    juice
1 measure grapefruit
    juice
1 measure coconut milk
pineapple wedge,
    to decorate

Put some crushed ice into a
cocktail shaker and pour in the
tequila, rum, pineapple and
grapefruit juices and coconut
milk. Shake the drink, then pour it
into a hurricane glass and
decorate with a pineapple wedge.
Serve with straws.

Serves 1

INDEX

NEW PHOTOGRAPHY
by William Reavell
Cocktails styled by Andrew
Fitz-Maurice at High Holborn,
95–96 High Holborn, London
WC1V 6LF

**ACKNOWLEDGEMENTS IN
SOURCE ORDER**

**Octopus Publishing Group
Limited**/ Neil Mersh 8, 11, 13,
17, 19, 21, 24, 27, 28, 31, 33,
34, 41, 45, 47, 50, 53, 63, 64,
67, 71, 73, 77, 87, 91/ Peter
Myers 6–7 background/ Sandra
Lane 3, 22/ William Reavell
front cover, back cover, 2, 5,
15, 38, 43, 55, 57, 59, 69, 75,
80, 83, 85, 89, 95